daddy cool

inspiring thoughts for fathers

www.youaretheauthor.com

Published in the UK in 2003 exclusively for
WHSmith Limited
Greenbridge Road
Swindon SN3 3LD
www.WHSmith.co.uk
by Tangent Publications, an imprint of
Axis Publishing Limited.

Conceived and created by
Axis Publishing Limited
8c Accommodation Road
London NW11 8ED
www.axispublishing.co.uk

Creative Director: Siân Keogh
Editorial Director: Brian Burns
Production Manager: Tim Clarke

ISBN 0-9543620-7-1

2 4 6 8 10 9 7 5 3 1

Printed and bound in China

about this book

Daddy Cool brings together an inspirational selection of powerful, life-affirming and humorous phrases about fathers and fatherhood, and combines them with evocative and gently amusing animal photographs that bring out the full comedy and pathos of the human condition.

We all lead busy lives and sometimes forget to tell our dads how much we love them and how grateful we are for everything they do for us. These inspiring examples of wit and wisdom, written by real people based on their true-life experiences, sum up the essence of fatherhood, and why our fathers will always have a special place in our hearts. As one of the entries so aptly puts it – a father is a banker provided by nature.

So give him a great big hug (then ask him for some money!)

about the author

Why have one author when you can have the world? This book has been

compiled using the incredible resource that is the world wide web. From the

many hundreds of contributions that were sent to the website,

www.youaretheauthor.com, we have selected the ones that best sum up what

being a dad is all about – giving support, encouragement and, most of all, love.

Please continue to send in your special views, feelings and advice about life –

you never know, you too might see your wise

words in print one day!

www.youaretheauthor.com

I'm just as lucky as I can
be for the world's coolest
dad belongs to me.

He is just the easiest person
to talk to and nothing ever seems
to surprise him.

anon@youaretheauthor.com

Any man can be a father. It takes someone special to be a dad.

To become a father is not hard. To be a father is, however.

Only when I got a little older did I realise that I'd given my dad an additional full-time occupation.

lucyclarke691@hotmail.com

It is easier for a father to have children than for children to have a real father.

You know when your dad is really there for you – it's not something you ever have to think about.

suphetty76@hotmail.com

Blessed indeed is
the man who hears
many gentle voices
call him father.

And he's blessed because
it's down to him that those
voices stay gentle.

anon@youaretheauthor.com

Children really
brighten up a
household.

They never turn
the lights off!

anon@youaretheauthor.com

It is a wise father who
knows his own child.

I used to think it strange that he
always seemed to know what I
wanted even before asking –
now I just think how lucky I am.

saffyshar@hotmail.com

A wise child maketh
a glad father.

anon@youaretheauthor.com

One father is worth
more than
a hundred
schoolmasters.

Others can teach you what
you know. A good father teaches
you how to be.

skinner_356@hotmail.com

Dad taught me
everything I know.
Unfortunately,
he didn't teach
me everything
he knows.

Thomas_Elliot@hotmail.com

Fathers send their
sons to college
either because they
went to college,
or because
they didn't.

anon@youaretheauthor.com

A dad is someone you look up to no matter how tall you are.

When in doubt – ask dad.

Even when he doesn't know,
at least he can say so and
point you in the direction of
someone who does.

lucyclarke691@hotmail.com

My father didn't tell me how to live; he lived, and let me watch him do it.

A father's good example is the best teacher.

Dad you're cool,
because although
you are silly,
you always look
after me when
I need you.

anon@youaretheauthor.com

I cannot think of any need in childhood as strong as the need for a father's protection.

He was the only one who could put the shadows away and scare off the wardrobe monster.

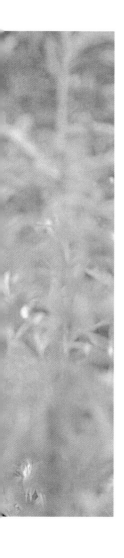

A man's children and his garden both reflect the amount of weeding done during the growing season.

anon@youaretheauthor.com

Fathers represent another
way of looking at life –
the possibility of an
alternative dialogue.

It's easy for a father to hear himself talking.

All he has to do is listen to his children!

What a father says to his children is not heard by the world, but it will be heard for posterity.

Dads give guidance for life
from your earliest days.

Dads – they say little, but give a lot.

A look, a simple look, can tell
me all I need to know.

mark.sit@lycos.com

The fundamental defect
of fathers is that they
want their children to
be a credit to them.

anon@youaretheauthor.com

A dad is a man who expects his son to be as good a man as he meant to be.

skinner_356@hotmail.com

By the time a man realizes that maybe his father was right, he usually has a son who thinks he's wrong.

As you get older, try to listen to your father more and judge less.

anon@youaretheauthor.com

Why are men reluctant to become fathers?

They aren't through being children yet.

stephanie_frances@yahoo.co.uk

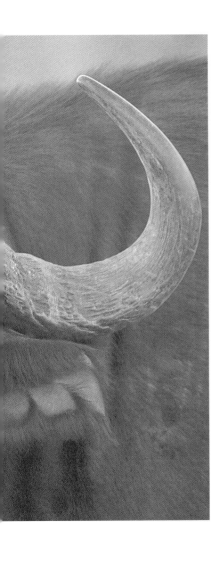

A truly great dad never puts away the simplicity of being a child.

If he did, how could he assemble
train sets on Christmas mornings
and play football in the
back garden?

The child had
every toy
his father wanted.

anon@youaretheauthor.com

There are three stages of a dad's life: he believes in Santa Claus, he doesn't believe in Santa Claus, he is Santa Claus.

Dad, you're sooooo embarrassing – but I love you.

Try to remember that, one day, you'll be wearing clothes that make your children cringe.

karen_smyth_107@hotmail.com

Having a family is like having a bowling alley installed in your head.

So just crack open a beer and
enjoy the game – it's not about to
end anytime soon.

anon@youaretheauthor.com

Bottle feeding: an opportunity for dad to get up at 2 am too.

Abi37@hotmail.com

Fatherhood is pretending the present you love the most is soap-on-a-rope.

anon@youaretheauthor.com

Q: What do you give the man who doesn't want anything?

A: Anything – he won't mind.

God can't fix everything…

…that's why he made dads, and he made them cool.

anon@youaretheauthor.com

My dad can do anything:
fix it if it's broken, grease it if
it's squeaky and build it if it
needs to be built.

Well, at least that's
what he thinks.

saramatthews12@hotmail.com

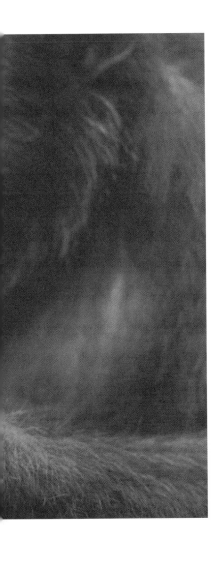

You know, dads just have a way of putting everything together.

Hell hath no fury
like a dad
whose tools are
messed up.

anon@youaretheauthor.com

When your dad is
mad at you and asks,
'Do I look stupid?'
don't answer him.

karen_smyth_107@hotmail.com

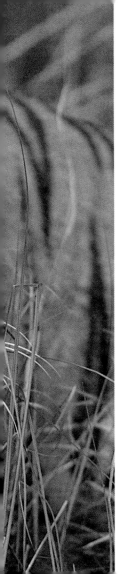

Love and fear.
Everything the father
of a family says must
inspire one or the other.

anon@youaretheauthor.com

The most important thing
a father can do for his children
is to love their mother.

anon@youaretheauthor.com

You don't have to deserve your mother's love.

You have to deserve your father's. He's more particular.

stephanie_frances@yahoo.co.uk

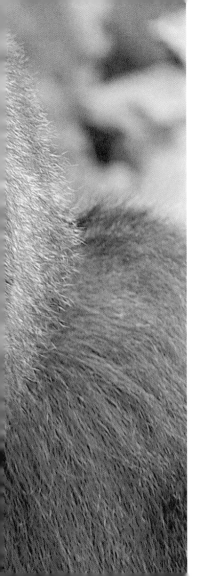

No child is
responsible
for his father.
That is entirely their
mother's affair.

anon@youaretheauthor.com

Dad is the boss in the house;
mum is just the decision maker.

Try to think of yourself as a
shareholder – even if it's just
a minority one!

suphetty76@hotmail.com

Mum says:
It's your decision.

Mum means:
The correct decision
should be obvious.

If mum is the storm,
then dad is the calm
afterwards.

In our house, the resolution to
many an argument begins with the
quietly spoken word, "Well…"

melanie_williams_2@hotmail.com

Dad is the keeper of keys; the lord of the airline tickets; the king of the amusement park passes, theatre tickets and hotel confirmation numbers.

Everyone knows that
Dad is little more than
chairman of the
entertainment committee.

For which I, for one, say "Hooray!
You can never have enough
entertainment."

mark.sit@lycos.com

Mum says to dad:
You have to learn to
communicate.

Mum means:
Just agree with me.

anon@youaretheauthor.com

Mum says to dad:
Do you love me?

Mum means:
I'm going to ask for
something expensive.

anon@youaretheauthor.com

Dad dreams, he plans, he struggles so that we might have the best.

A father is a banker provided by nature.

But be careful — no bank
is a bottomless pit.

lucyclarke391@hotmail.com

You can always rely on dad cabs – twenty-four hour call-out, and no meter.

Never lend your
car to anyone
to whom you
are a dad.

Geoffrey_Howarth@hotmail.com

That is the thankless position of the father in the family: the provider for a bunch of ingrates.

anon@youaretheauthor.com

It is admirable for a man to take his son fishing, but there is a special place in heaven for the cool dad who takes his daughter shopping.

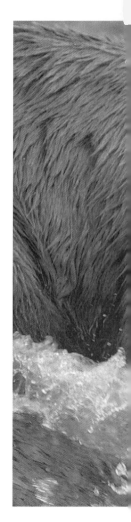

saramatthews12@hotmail.com

A cool dad is a guy who has snapshots in his wallet where his money used to be.

And they're probably snapshots of you, so bear it in mind the next time you ask for money.

anon@youaretheauthor.com

A truly rich man
is one whose
children run into
his arms when his
hands are empty.

karen_smyth_107@hotmail.com

Sometimes the poorest
man leaves his children
the richest inheritance.

It's called love, so remember
to pass it on.

anon@youaretheauthor.com

My dad gave me
the greatest gift
anyone could give
another person:
he believed in me.

The greatest gift I ever had…

he is really cool… I call him Dad.

anon@youaretheauthor.com